SHADES OF BROWN

In memory of my grandmother,

Evalee Hazel Claytor-

"We were all once beautiful flowers."

SHADES
OF
BROWN

BY
MERCEDES WEATHERS

Library of Congress Cataloging in Publication Data

Weathers, Mercedes
Shades of Brown
ISBN: 978-1-54398-189-6

Printed in The United States of America

BOOK DESIGN BY MERCEDES WEATHERS

this book is dedicated to

black girls weathering the storms through the soul's eye

M.W.

CONTENTS

BLACK GIRLS

BROWN GIRL

i have no king to call my own
so i will build my own castle
to be queen

i have no king to call my own
he is gone
or perhaps
he never came
i have surrendered to the thought
of perhaps
running this monarchy
alone
i look to my sisters for strength
Deborah, Priscilla, Makeda, Esther, Naomi

my garden is overflowing
waiting to be watered
by other hands
i have no king to call my own
but my castle is strong
with a fortress of God

i have no king to call my own
but welcome to my castle

ACCEPT HER FATE

no one told them not to sing
they just stopped

one day
walking down the street
she saw a flower so beautiful
a melody danced before her eyes
and when she opened her mouth
to swallow it
it ran as if it wanted her to follow
but she gave up

when the needle pierced her finger
she didn't cry out
but kept sewing
drops of blood soaking
the stainless, pure white cloth
she didn't care
the beauty of the work had been
destroyed

but this object must be completed
to cloak her body in this light garment
to hide the burden of her soul

and when it was finished
she wore it
and felt the same heaviness

it wasn't until she heard

the song one day

bursting through the peaceful surroundings

of her world

that she understood

and decided to take singing lessons

BLACK MAN

hey black man

there were so many things

i wanted to say

but

i was so mesmerized

by your chocolate brown skin

so mesmerized

by the flow of seductive words coming from your mouth

that i didn't

so invited by the kiss you blew

that i acted like i didn't see

so excited by the rhythm in your walk

the air of nonchalant power

that i really wanted to touch

to take that warm softness inside

to cushion it with love

so much

but instead

i kept walking

BLACK, BROWN, BEIGE – IN THE MIDDLE

not coffee, chocolate, sand-colored or wheat

just

hey, brown girl

the color of earth

chocolate with a little bit of cream

coffee with a little bit of milk

that color in between

just noticeable enough to be camouflaged

with the red bones, high yellows, and dark chocolate

i stand

floating between ashes and dust

i am not biracial

i am racial

a blending of many

uncomplaining against

the trauma of being dark

or the privileges of being light

"if you black, jump back

if you brown…"

hey, that's me

that color blending together two

sides

the safe color

feeling it all

invisible

because i am brown

FLOWERS

there are many different
flowers
of all shades and hues
but they are all mine

flowers sometimes bud on the front step
talking loud talking bad
to chase away the fear
hidden deep within their souls

flowers are sometimes weighed
down by the pressure of brothers
who cannot carry the burden of their own soul

flowers are sometimes picked apart
petal by petal
by a society which says
they are ugly on the streets
but beautiful in the beds

flowers are often
hidden in the shade
dumped in the alleys
attempting to nourish their roots
with their own tears of life

flowers wilt under the depression
of a false love
and sometimes seek sunlight in the arms of a white man

all these flowers are in me

and i say

you may be picked, plucked, wilted or malnourished

but you will never die

GRANDMA

when she first told me
i didn't believe it would happen

later the tears rushed down
as if they had been waiting
for such a long time

they tried to chase away the pain
of stored memories,
pickled watermelon rinds,
and clothes for
Barbie
but i ran
hoping to catch a last glimpse of
your shadow

and it wasn't until
i felt the wetness on my cheek
that i understood

GRATITUDE FOR LONELINESS

those were the days

i may one day say

as i reminisce

on the feeling of

my thighs caressing

one another

lying beside no one else

the feeling of my arms

wrapped around

me

securely

because my want, desire

was stronger than my reality

thinking of who would be next

after me

who would take my place

holding me with

love

who would make me stop

thinking

so that now as i lie here

feeling you beside

me

i say

those were the days

ICE EYES

hold me

said my eyes

but his voice said it wasn't good

so i went the other way

laugh said my spirit

but it was stiff and didn't come from

the soul

whenever i laughed

people would look at me

as if to say

you

with the brown eyes, brown skin

with that peaceful placidity-

that is what they saw-

how could you laugh

open

with such

life

stopped between us

and i didn't ask anymore

until my softness froze in his

presence

it wasn't until i realized

that the flame was

in me that i adjusted the temperature

to start a slow simmer

and let my heart emanate

to melt the distance

GO SISTER GIRL

when you ask-

did you see that girl
with the big mouth
and small doubts
with the big reason
for the little dream
of being recognized
for what she is
what is she?
she looks like
just some brown girl
but she is so much more
if you ask her
she may say "nothing"
but she sure walks down the street
like the president
and don't let her start talking
'cause she may not stop

so that day
when you asked
i did not know
because to me
that's just my girl

INNER VOICE

BODY TALK

hey
how you doin'
sweet thang
mmm……
lookin' good enough to eat
you a model?
ain't never seen no one as fine as you
you got a man?
i know if you was mine
you'd be smilin' everyday
with a smile like that
what's your name?
hello?
can't you speak?
i said, what's your name?
what's your problem?
your man don't treat you right?
or you just stuck up
i see you got them books
you think you more educated than me
maybe if you smiled more
you wouldn't look half as bad
i don't know who you think you is
with your stank attitude

BODY LANGUAGE

you know at first
i was going to smile
but then i thought
i don't know you
and i don't want to

i sometimes wonder
why can't i walk down the street
i mean a friendly hello is fine
but if i don't answer back
isn't that my prerogative
is a smile sufficient?
so anyway
i kept walking
and as i thought
of what my grandmother's grandmother
went through
so that i could walk down the street
with pride
i thought
i don't owe you nothing

MICHELLE

her skin was dark brown

i saw your lips form the words

describing Michelle-

and then

this other one

you say

is attractive

but all i remember is a blond, amazon white girl

no comparison

to the beautiful strength

of Michelle

her dark brown skin smooth and glowing

and in anger i recall yesterday

when you mentioned Michelle-

a fragment in your mind-

as that dark skinned girl

PRELUDE TO A FIRST KISS

my first
impressions
were not that
good
was not a word for
you
just another playboy
i thought
and i stared at the smooth, brown
skin
mesmerized by the
lips
friendly eyes
looked at
me
and when you kissed me
i stood there waiting
expecting
for the possession
wanting the caress of your lips against
mine

feeling your soft firmness leaving me
i realized that although this was only
a goodbye to you
to me this was the beginning of
expectation
aroused by an eagerly awaited
joy

SISTER

of course i didn't know it then

or perhaps i did

sometimes we know things

deep down in our subconscious

like when you know it's going to snow

from a smell or a feel

but don't really acknowledge it

yet the softened ice

brushes against your cheek

without shock or surprise

and this is how i felt about you

as i

followed the turn of the bicycle wheels

the backwards glance of your eyes

the side to side upward sway of your shoulders

so it came as no surprise

when one day i looked up to see

the shadow of your embrace

reaching out to me as i rode ahead

THE FRIEND

well
i guess
it's kind of like
two trees
growing on the same land
side by side
they both have seeds
different
but the same
they both have fruit
just different
sometimes if it rains too much for one
the roots soak up the extra moisture
or if there is too much sun
one shades the other
or sometimes
each just stands
alone
it seemed
we were like this
and our laughter kept us from
rotting
so that we could still stand if our fruitfulness seemed to fall

from a distance these two trees can
look
so similar
but if you come close
you see they are so different

but yet their roots have grown together

over the years

i guess this is how we were

maybe

THE POND

and now i am a pond
reflecting
so dutifully the image that comes
to greet me each day

she rushes out with
eager anticipation
and lets out a light sigh
as she gently caresses her cheek
relieved that i have not yet
betrayed her secret
of the young girl who she has
drowned
but unaware of the vulnerability
grown out of many used days
which emerges from my depths

WEATHERING THE STORMS

VISION QUEST

holding me so closely
i thought it was a dream

the morning i woke up
screaming
with joy
was that this feeling
of running to a cliff
and yelling your name
even though you were
standing
behind me
lies the secrets, lies, shame
of the past

i awoke to the cry of
birds
flying over the mountains
and i realized
that i was free

A PIECE OF NOTHINGNESS

i like the peace of nothingness
the feel of the air
between your legs

the sound of the silence
underneath the distant lawnmower

the realization
that you have no lover
and do not need one
because it is not time

the clink of the melting ice
in the glass

the cleanness
of moving on

the decision
of not caring

but most of all
the nothingness of
this moment

DRY POPCORN

this feeling
which suddenly appears
like the never forgotten
spirit
of a dead lover
releases a joy of
being
filled with
sunlight hazes-
transferring her to
a daze-like
existence
in which she could feel
the slightest summer breeze
against her eyelids

she
who had
known of
death
some short
time ago
now knew life

a short distance of time
before
she had yearned for the
feel
taste

smell

of hot buttered popcorn-

a promise

which had been given

the night before she had

dreamt of the promise

and awoke with

remaining salt

still on her hands

particles of freedom in her mind

when the silver lined bag was given

and she could actually touch

the unbuttered dryness

she felt the dry kernels against her lips

and she was not disappointed

at the unexpected surprise

for she realized that the joy she felt was

You

FOR THE SAKE OF A PEN

perhaps they assumed
i
did not have a pen
sitting here
scrunched across from
one white man
next to
a white man
and diagonal from
a white woman
i wonder
what i appear to be like
with my
brown skin
it is clear to me
that my eyes were open
when the question was asked
"do you have a pen?"

but i was bypassed
not that i would look for
a pen
perhaps it was for the sake
of this white woman that i was
overlooked
perhaps my pen was not good enough
or perhaps i was really, truly not seen
so i closed my eyes
opting to be blind

to their closed minds

and opening them

i decided not to put the same energy

to care about them

that they put into their fear of me

and i took out my pen

to write these

words

ON MUSEUMS AND CHURCHES

when i walk into

a church

the feeling i feel

is very similar

to being in a museum

an alive inspired happiness

of holding hands with grandma

of smiling into the eyes of a friend

for no reason

of laughing at nothing

of swinging hands with my mother

in the rain

memories which remain in the mind

of a girl

but which have helped me become

a woman

D-DAY REVISITED

too much has already happened

for me

to know

to understand

what is going on inside of me

too much has already happened

for me

to know

that you

mainly see my imperfections

too much

for me to feel linked to your

impressive words

for me to be impressed by

your worldliness

for me to see anything

but your soul

for me to want anything

but your truth

for me to feel connected

in this room of people

to know that we

lie

in the same blood, same clothes, same skin

but

too much has already happened

and i thought i had

forgotten

but it is with me

even when i forget it

i still feel the hole where

the needle pierced my soul

and i try to cover it up

and say that it is not there

but it has already happened

INTERPRETATION OF A SECOND

she was awakened

each day

by the soft caress

of a warm glow

filling her body

so completely with a joy

she could not explain

to me

the dreams of a young girl

too complex to even trace in

the mind

the revisions of the past and

longings for the future

PRIDE COMETH AFTER A FALL

i walk proud
because my ancestors couldn't
but still did

i walk proud
so that my people will be

i walk proud
because i know i am loved

because i make mistakes
and still have the strength to walk

because i have been chosen
for the fight that lies before me

i walk proud
because i will be
because i am not

because i am
because you live in me

SPLIT SECOND REVOLUTION

i saw it all so clearly

without looking

the khaki colored

trench raincoat

the flat style-less shoes

the pink shaded lipstick

i saw this all

in the corner of my eye

while looking straight ahead

i saw the frozen expression

of closed distant resistance

and the white skin

i wondered briefly

what you saw

but didn't really care

ever so often

i am struck by what "your kind"

think of

me

i sense

your fear

your inferiority

your jealousy

your liberal minded acceptance

your hatred

your attraction

and then i see

once again

all that i represent

for i not only represent

what you aren't

but what you want to be

but in this phase of the game

when i saw you

i was just walking down the street

i took it all in

your quick small steps

i even saw the way you inched over

so that you were directly in my path

or perhaps you thought

it was your path

did you think i would move?

did you think i would lower my head in shame?

or perhaps cowardly mumble an apology

or maybe even rear up in an attack

the moment of truth had arrived

and here i stand

staring directly into your frozen eyes

knowing i would not move

you said excuse me

and shuffled around

me

my pathway was momentarily cleared

and although i realized that only one stone

had been kicked to the gutter

and many more would attempt to trip me

i also realized that

stones were made for walking on

SUBWAY OF LIFE

beauty is only skin deep
you are only as beautiful as you feel
beauty is in the eye of the beholder
cliches which have become
memorized reassurances for
future disappointments
of unknown ridicule, unfulfilled love and other empty spaces
which have caused me to ignore pains
buried deep within my heart

and so life
had become a series of emotional challenges
where looking into one's eyes was a great feat
where trauma was caused by letting someone too close
to a place which wanted to be held, caressed
loved

daily staring into this
deceptive glass
which served no better purpose
than to hide her
true beauty
clearly showing the image
which the world saw
her brown skin

my ancestors
are people who i have

never seen

but have felt

walking through familiar hallways

and stairs of sadness

i wonder what these others

see in me that i

don't see

do see

the door shuts

as she glances

seemingly without interest

quickly around the crowded

underground passage of disinterested faces

eyes taking in her small smile

miss

her truth

as she takes in

the poetry in motion

THE FUTURE

and what shall i be

when i am alone

and love is no longer a dream

shall i smile

against the sadness inside

or let everyone see

the pain

shall i truly believe

this is my destiny

and not just

something in need of

acceptance

like the child amongst strangers

doing anything for attention

a spilled glass of milk

a broken plate

are these all innocent of fate

or some subconscious

predetermined energy

making its way into this world

is this what causes the pain

you are a stranger within my soul

i refused so long

to give you the permission of this address

but now all letters have been returned to sender

too often

and there is no other forwarding destination

before i only thought of you

with positive rebellion

but now i see your

truth

and in that there is some comfort

for once i allow myself to be

your friend

perhaps then i will smile anyway

THE NEW WORLD

stop

the fact being
it was a lie
unknowingly given
innocently accepted
ears willingly ate
brain digested
I WILL TRAVEL THE WORLD
SEEK NEW PEOPLES
BASK IN THE SUNLIT PASTURES
but when the messenger came
he did not bear gifts of great rewards
the reward had already been given
and now it was time to pay

TRIBAL FLOW

i see you watching
and know
how you love to hate

the effervescence of
the eye
shines deeper
than the womb of nature
hey
what do you see
when i see you
seeing
my black skin
brown eyes
the secret
that i am
woman
waiting to embrace
all

if you look
deeply
you may see
the sycamore tree
waving in the breeze
hips flowing in sunlit places
or maybe you will see
me

THROUGH THE SOUL'S EYE

THE LETTER

Hey…did you see that girl walking down the street….with the spring in her step…yeah, that was me….with the pretty dress…with the glowing light….with the spirit that jumps with the breezes….yeah, my skirt was tight, but that don't matter….did you see my eyes…full with the love of God….did you see my smile blowing away long forgotten sadness….did you see my swinging arms welcoming the trials and fun of tomorrow…did you see that girl in the red dress….that's right…it was me….and if you don't know, you better ask someone…..did you see the letter in my hand…that I dropped…in the mailbox….it was to you…..asking you….to come join me….on this wild journey called life…with God as our guide

HOPSCOTCH

playing hopscotch is the way some people love

one foot

two feet

one foot

two

whoops you missed

playing with friends on a hot

sticky day

i looked for my special stone

to throw on my designated number

this balancing act can be so tricky

but yet so fun

is this feeling love

or life

or neither

once i reach ten

and turn around

i've come so far

and now that i'm almost home and won the game

should i go play rope?

no, i'll stick to the game i've chosen

THE ONION LOVER

i don't love onions
because they make my taste buds come alive with flavor
or because their endless rings
resemble the circles of life
or because they release
tears from my eyes that have
been held back
forever
or because they are pulled from the earth
from which i came
or even because of
the crisp, clean sound they make
as they are being sliced, diced and chopped

i only love onions
because they remind me of
my mother

GENESIS

i have told you all
and do not want to go back
the initial blending of longing, and anxiety
of telling my past
has dissipated

all that remains is a fear
of leaving the door open in the dark
for we are still in the dark
and i do not know if i should leave
the door
open or shut

i have told you my story
and you have told me yours
i no longer know where yours begins
and mine ends
they have blended together
and in fear
i reach to grab mine back
before the door closes
and we are left here
alone
together
when i realize that i no longer
want the story back

and i surrender
to pleasure amalgamation

BASKING IN ROBIN

i walked into the store not knowing
what flavor to pick
i didn't know just what i wanted
just something that warmed me
with its cool firmness
to fill my every being
every crevice
yearning
for something yet unknown
so when i saw the mango berry
i knew this was the one
without knowing why
forgetting precaution
no hesitant taster spoon was required
dispelling thoughts of wastefulness
which would only bear a single scoop
i asked for a double
i knew i would want more
without knowing why
because i don't like mango
and i don't like berry
but i sure like mango-berry
and this is why i say
i didn't choose you

DON"T FORGET TO BRING A SWEATER

why did you say

i was like the deepest
blue sky
that you wanted to lose yourself
inside of me- that you
wanted to enter the deepness
and go further
inside

why did you say

you wanted to stop
but you couldn't

why did you say
that one day
you would take me to the Rhine- that you
could see me
in a get-away cabin in the woods
who would i be with?

why did you say things
that made me feel special
when i don't know how to hold
this feeling

why did you rub my heart

after i had already put on
my winter coat

FRIEND

and now that you've seen past
the brown in my skin
the gaze in my eyes
the hope in my sigh
the daydream in my thoughts

do you see me
like i see you

the faith in your laughter
the love in your hugs
the color of your soul
or do you just
see me

GOD'S LOVE

it rushes by so quickly sometimes

that i almost see its edge

although i feel its core so deeply

like the time when we were driving

so quickly

that we forgot to stop

and i screamed out

in laughter

or fear?

and then the moment was gone

but you were still there

or like the times

when i've sat

so alone

on this rock

warmed by the heat of the sun

alone but not alone

like the way i feel your arms surrounding me

when i wake up

and then realize that it is my blanket

or is it?

like the point when i realize

i am not running because of me

but because you are pushing me on

like the times that i have cried in pain

because the hurt was too deep

to comfort myself

like the time

i felt your love

I DIDN'T KNOW

i didn't know that

no

you mean to tell me

that all that time

and you didn't even tell me

i wish i had known

i could have done something

i know i would have said something

something

dang

if i had known

i can't believe you didn't tell me

you told who?

i would have thought that you would have told me if anyone

but you didn't

true

you did now

but so much time

so much time

if you had told me

i could have done something

something

like

told you too

MY FRIEND

if i had known
that you would make
me laugh
at times when i thought i would cry
perhaps i would have kept you close to my heart

if i had known
that i could look into your eyes
and see a joke
before it was born
maybe i would have grasped your friendship by the hand

if i had known
that my soul would smile
whenever you were in my minds eye

perhaps then
i would have understood
friendship

perhaps that is why
i am here
telling you this now

because i did

DAYDREAMING WITH DADDY

when i think of jazz
i think of being downtown
holding hands
with my dad
on a lazy Saturday afternoon
summer days
shirley temples at Charlie's
sitting in on sets
at Ortlieb's
sweeping the street
after my dad mowed the lawn
sitting in the back seat
my sister and me
listening to
my father
listening to the music
i wondered
how long i would remember
this song
this moment
this jazz
my dad

I CRIED A RIVER

i cried a river……

the day i realized the truth……
that this place called life………..
was one battle after the next…….that the fight became more once i
knew this…..
i cried a river over you

i cried a river ……
when i realized that i could not be like you….
that my hair was thick and wild…….
that my heart showed too easily in my eyes……
i cried a river over you
and then i stopped……..
and cried some more when i understood

i cried a river when i saw that you were just a disguise…..
that what i thought i saw…….i didn't…..
that what i thought you saw…..you couldn't….
that you just saw my shell….
i cried a river…..
when i cut my hair…..
when you missed me singing….
when i waited for you….
when you didn't come….
when i was forgotten….
i cried a river…..
and then i went to work

TEATIME

love came to my door today

with a cupful of sugar

i opened the door and said

come in

i had tea on to boil

and when it was steeped

the aroma floating softly

over its golden brown taste

i set the teacups down

ready to share this gift

he stirred in the sugar

and we watched as it dissolved

its sweetness forever taken

i lifted the cup to his

lips

but when he felt the heat

i saw the fear and love

blending in a swirl of

emotional flavor

and not knowing what to do

i moved the cup away

for him to try another day

THE CODE

i lost my heart the other day
and now i can't find my keys
will you point me in
the right direction
of the lost and found
or at least
give me that chain you wear
around your neck
with the gold key
dangling between the softness
that blankets your chest
is it mine?
or yours
i do not know
you use it so freely
to unlock my goodness

why have you given me this key
to open your heart?
but when the door is open
you only let me peek inside
i hear the rhythm of the
blowing fan
the warmth circulating towards me
why have you given me this key
and coded your soul
with this alarm of lust
the sound is so piercing

so strong

blending in syncopation

with all i contain

the sound has enraptured me

and is now fading in the distance

far away

for i have immersed myself

in you

or have you come into

me

i cannot tell

for i have found

that the alarm has stopped

and the code

was my love

THE QUESTION OF LOVE

asking me

why

is like asking me if i want more

pineapple

it is fruitless

knowing as you do

how i love

everything about it

cutting away its protective cover

slicing away the sweet juicy fruit from the

core

my favorite part

which i will save until last

i gorge myself with it

eating one piece after another

and when i'm done

i even like

the numbing of my taste buds

so that i can taste nothing

but pineapple

for this is all i want to taste

so if you ask me why

there really is no answer

i just do

THE UNDERSTANDING

when he used to say
i want you to meet my daughter
he did not say
how beautiful she was
or all the interesting things she did
so i walked into the situation
unknowing, unexpecting

it was not until
i met her
that i realized
that it did not matter
for she was his daughter
and he was her father

WOULD I, WILL I, DO I

no one told me you would be the same in my heart

ten years from then

or that you'd smell the same

like the water washing off

of the banks of the river

the same river that i bathed with my tears

trying to blend

with you

to grasp you

in some way

no one told me that you would taste the same

like dry, salty alcohol

that your eyes would look the same

empty but deep

like there was something there that you didn't want me to see

that you'd have the same slow shift to your walk

that you would still cock your head up to answer

a question

that you would still shrug off a question with a short laugh

that i would still know the truth of your lies and listen

that i could still see your smile and awaken

that you would still do the things that i hated to love

that you could still be you

WITH A TWIST-ON THE ROCKS

i don't call it love

and he doesn't say

'cause he doesn't know

doesn't care

doesn't

he plays love with someone

then he plays games with other women's

bodies

hearts

souls

well, that's love

with a twist

of lemon

it grows sour in time

rocky as the ice in this

empty glass

so that she

and she

and she

and me?

i don't think so

are left waiting

for the rocky times

to melt and

take a sip of love

i'd rather have a smooth glass of water

'cause i like my love

straight up

IT'S TIME FOR A REVOLUTION

it's time for a revolution
of standing for the truth
and doing it

it's time for a revolution
of feeling the power that surges in your blood
and knowing that it comes from your blessing
and not your doing

it's time for a revolution
of the knowledge that no one
owes you anything

it's time for a revolution
of marching towards victory
with the pride of a job well done

it's time for a revolution
of wearing my hair wild and wooly
or straight and smooth
not to make a statement
but because it looks beautiful

it's time for a revolution
of men who stand up for their women
and women who stand up for their men

it's time for a revolution

of thought shown in actions

it's time for a revolution
of men who prove their love with unadulterated actions
of women who don't give in to false love

of people who love through sacrifice

of me saying the truth
and you listening